PUPPIES
AS A NEW PET

JAMES MICHAELSON

CONTENTS

Photographs by Dr. Herbert R. Axelrod, Isabelle Francais, Ron Reagan, Vincent Serbin, and Sally Anne Thompson.

Distributed in the UNITED STATES by T.F.H. Publications, Inc., One T.F.H. Plaza, Neptune City, NJ 07753; in CANADA to the Pet Trade by H & L Pet Supplies Inc., 27 Kingston Crescent, Kitchener, Ontario N2B 2T6; Rolf C. Hagen Ltd., 3225 Sartelon Street, Montreal 382 Quebec; in CANADA to the Book Trade by Macmillan of Canada (A Division of Canada Publishing Corporation), 164 Commander Boulevard, Agincourt, Ontario M1S 3C7; in ENGLAND by T.F.H. Publications, The Spinney, Parklands, Portsmouth PO7 6AR; in AUSTRALIA AND THE SOUTH PACIFIC by T.F.H. (Australia) Pty. Ltd., Box 149, Brookvale 2100 N.S.W., Australia; in NEW ZEALAND by Ross Haines & Son, Ltd., 82 D Elizabeth Knox Place, Panmure, Auckland, New Zealand; in the PHILIPPINES by Bio-Research, 5 Lippay Street, San Lorenzo Village, Makati, Rizal; in SOUTH AFRICA by Multipet Pty. Ltd., P.O. Box 35347, Northway, 4065, South Africa. Published by T.F.H. Publications, Inc. Manufactured in the United States of America by T.F.H. Publications, Inc.

DEDICATION

This little book is dedicated to all the puppies who have made a youngster's life more complete.

BEFORE WE BEGIN

Sharing your home and life with a dog is truly one of the most rewarding pet experiences; and beginning these years of commitment by raising and training your dog from puppyhood surely provides the most possible enrichment of the entire pet encounter. This book prepares the new owner with a groundwork of information concerning the selection, the basic and higher needs of the puppy, early training and lead training, housebreaking, and an overview of the development of the puppy, from birth to one year.

SELECTION

Selecting *your* dog involves a very subjective, personal decision process. With over 400 purebreds and countless crossbreeds and mongrels, the dog world today opens the kennel to the potential owner to purchase the dog that ideally fills his needs and expectations. While it is surely beyond the scope of this book to discuss every type of dog, the author realizes that the first and possibly most formidable task of the prospective puppy owner is selection, and hence we begin with an overview of the world of dogs.

The mixed breed or mongrel—call it what you will—has been championed by many as the best kind of canine you could ever want.

PUREBRED -VS- MONGREL

Perhaps the first delineation made of the world's dogs is between purebred and mongrel. For most purposes, a purebred dog is one that traces a pure lineage through both parents back at least to the day the breed was recognized by a registering body. A pure lineage refers to descent in which all members of the "family" were members of the respective breed. This lineage must trace back to the day (or year) in which the breed was recognized, excepting breeds for which there are acceptable outcrosses. The American Kennel Club (AKC) is the largest registering body in America, while the Kennel Club of Great Britain (KCGB) holds the same distinction on the British Isles. The Federation Cynologique Internationale is considered the registering body for Continental Europe, as well as numerous other countries, including Mexico. All purebred dogs should be registered with an appropriate registering body. Information about the following kennel clubs and their registration policies can be

acquired by writing to:

- American Kennel Club, 51 Madison Avenue, New York, NY 10010
- Australian National Kennel Club, Administrative Buildings, Royal Showgrounds, Ascot Vale 3032, Victoria
- Canadian Kennel Club, 2150 Bloor Street West, Toronto, Ontario M6S 4V7
- Federation Cynologique Internationale, Rue Leopold-II, 14B-6530 Thuin, Belgium
- The Kennel Club (Great Britain), 1-5 Clarges Street, London W1Y 8AB, England
- United Kennel Club, 100 East Kilgore Road, Kalamazoo, MI 49001-5597

A mongrel, on the other hand, is a dog without pure descent. For the purposes of most kennel clubs, the "impurity" may be the result of one mating or many. For example, a cross between a purebred Cocker Spaniel and a purebred Poodle, resulting in the popular crossbred known as the "Cockapoo," is considered simply a mongrel by the major registering bodies. The essential reason is that no dogs but purebreds reproduce with a degree of reliability demanded of the various registering organizations. In other words, purebreds breed true, while all others—crossbreds included—do not. Though the term "mongrel" may have a slightly denigrating connotation, the mongrel dog is most always a fine example of the canine, having all those doggie traits of affection, loyalty, etc., even if occurring in a less-than-predictable body type.

A British spaniel-type dog. If you are interested in pursuing a show career for your purebred pup, it goes without saying that he should be of good conformation for his breed.

If you plan to be a show person or breeder, then there is no question that you want a registered purebred dog. If, however, you simply desire a companion, especially a low-cost companion,   a mongrel may be the best option. Either way, if your sole desire is a dog, you can't go wrong, for on the inside a dog is a dog is a dog.

WHICH BREED FOR YOU

Pardoning the last statement about a dog being a dog, potential dog owners must be aware that each breed, and indeed each individual dog, has a temperament of its own. Therefore, without being too idealistic, the best beginning to the selection process is determining which dog type, referring to what *kind* of dog, you wish to own, based upon the general temperament, characteristics, and needs of the breed and your own needs and offerings. In general, the many purebred dogs of the world can be grouped into categories, based on their abilities,

derivation, and development. Not surprisingly, most breeds that share a category also share similar physical traits and behavioral characteristics. For example, in the category known as the hound group, most breeds have short coats, drop ears, excellent sense of smell, and generally a calm demeanor. Beginning with the general canine groups allows the purchaser to focus on breeds which fit well into the apartment, set stately and impressive as home guardians, delight the children with unending hours of romping and play, retrieve felled game for the hunting enthusiast, or

6

perform any of many numerous other functions.

Unquestionably, a brief study of the canine "groups" greatly assists in the search for the right breed. (Incidentally, most mongrels and crossbreds demonstrate characteristics and general appearance not too foreign from the general type evidenced in the various groups. Therefore, if you wish to purchase a mongrel, it still pays to understand the various canine groupings.)

The nine canine groups are: mastiffs, sighthounds, flockguards, herding dogs, hounds, gundogs, nordic dogs, terriers, and toy dogs. Note that this categorization differs from the group system employed by the AKC, KCGB, and many other kennel clubs: whereas their categorization primarily is to expedite judging at dog shows, the group system employed in this book is most efficient for describing general shared traits and characteristics.

The mastiffs are typically large, fearless dogs with big hearts and big appetites. Mastiffs almost invariably prove good guard dogs, composed of strong bone and abundant muscle; mastiffs are

renowned for their bonding closely to the human family. To better understand this group, three sub-categories can be created: the "true" mastiffs, the draft/cattle dogs, and the bulldogs. The mastiffs include the Rottweiler, Boxer, Bulldog, English Mastiff, Great Dane, Saint Bernard, Newfoundland, American Pit Bull Terrier, Doberman Pinscher, and many others. Many of the mastiffs were created for different purposes: some to hunt, some to guard, others to rescue in snow or water. Of course, these differences in development need to be taken into account by the potential owner. Yet,

Old English Sheepdog puppy. Members of this breed are intelligent and affectionate and can make a fine housepet.

Lovely headstudy of a Mastiff pup.

choosing among the mastiff breeds generally assures one an impressively composed animal, typically calm and fearless, willing to sacrifice all for the well-being of its human family. Mastiffs invariably demand obedience training and plenty of room and time for exercise.

The sighthounds are typically

long-legged, sleek, muscular dogs, which may tend towards the aloof and require considerable exercise. Many of the sighthounds are quite ancient breeds, their friezes coursing Pharaoh's tombs. For centuries the sighthounds have been dogs of the nobility, gracing castles of kings and czars and coursing wolf, boar, and hare during the royal hunt. Sighthounds are dogs of the wind, the course, the race; they include the Greyhound, Whippet, Afghan Hound, Irish Wolfhound, Scottish Deerhound, Whippet, and Rhodesian Ridgeback, to name a few. Sighthounds make great companions but are usually quite wary of strangers. They require a lot of exercise and are best kept in homes with large

yards in which to chase and play. Two sighthounds is often better than one, as the two will keep each other active in the yard and thereby happier dogs in the home. Coursing events are increasing in popularity in the U.S. and around the world. Sighthound owners can consider participation in these most exciting events.

The flock guards, somewhat like the mastiffs, were bred for courage, strength, and tenacity. Their original occupation remains their group name: guardians of shepherd's flocks. The flock guards, once combating wolves on the Russian steppes and Hungarian plains, are necessarily large, imposing animals. Most, but by no means all, flock guards are

The puppy you select should be alert and interested in the goings-on around him.

A pair of Whippet pups. Selecting the dog breed that is right for you goes far beyond good looks: character and personality are vital considerations when making your choice.

covered with a dense, white, flowing coat. The flock guard's coat was one of its most vital features, protecting the animal from the winds and rains of the wild and the jagged teeth of predators. The flock guards are stately dogs, best known for their close, absolute bonding with human family members. Member flock guardians include: the Kuvasz, Komondor, Great Pyrenees, Anatolian Shepherd Dog, and many others. Flock guards demand spacious living quarters and are best kept away from neighbors dogs—especially any rather wolflike ones. Obedience training and exercise are also requisites of responsible ownership.

The herding dogs are typically active, athletic, remarkably intelligent dogs with an unstinted instinct to herd. Herding dogs vary in size from the rather small Welsh Corgis to the rather large German Shepherd Dog and Old English Sheepdog. Their coat types and colors also vary considerably, from long, to short, to wire, to goat; from merle, to bicolor, to solid. Other members of the herding group include the Bouvier des Flandres, Briard, Bearded Collie, Collie, and Shetland Sheepdog, to list but a few. The herding dogs are true workers, forever willing to give 100 percent of themselves to meet the needs of their owner.

Herding dogs typically make great companions and can be trained to almost any task, clearly evidenced in the multi-functional German Shepherd Dog.

The scenthounds, or simply hounds, range in size from the smaller bassets and beagles to the larger braques and coonhounds. Most hounds have short coats, drop ears, and full voice;

many have abundant wrinkles of skin. The scenthounds are typically dogs of the hunt, bred to track deer, otter, and raccoon for centuries, though in recent years many a Basset Hound, Beagle, Black and Tan, and Bloodhound have found their welcome way into pet homes as solely companions. The hounds generally make excellent companions, gentle and easy in temperament, though some breeds are too intensely the hunter and really deserve hunting owners. The hounds are hearty dogs, most being suited to either indoor or outdoor life. Hounds love to riot in the woods and delight in exercise hours with the owner. Hounds respond excellently to training, and outdoors enthusiasts can consider participation in field trials if they purchase a hound.

The gundogs include some of the most popular of all dog breeds, including the Poodle, Cocker Spaniel, and Labrador Retriever. The gundogs carry

Familiarizing yourself with the different canine groups will help you decide which group you would like your dog to come from and will narrow down your choice to a smaller number of breeds.

11

The nordic breeds are typically plushly coated dogs with prick ears and curled tail. As suggested in their name, the nordic dogs descend from the north, where their ancestors pulled sleds, herded reindeer, and hunted game. Breeds included in the nordic group are the Siberian Husky, Alaskan Malamute, Chinook, Chow Chow, Samoyed, and Finnish Spitz, to name a few of the better known ones. The nordic dogs make tireless companions and are very social and pack oriented, fitting well into the human family structure. Owners living is warm climates must use caution that their northern dog not become overheated. Exercise requirements for most nordic dogs are very high.

their name because these breeds were originally bred to hunt from the gun: to point, flush, set, and retrieve. Thus we have the sub-categories of pointers, flushers (springers and cockers), setters, and retrievers. A representative from each of the respective sub-categories could be the German Wirehaired Pointer, English Springer and English Cocker Spaniels, Irish Setter, and Golden Retriever. Gundogs are renowned for their affection, intelligence and trainability. The gundogs are typically gentle and make fine companions for children. Gundogs do require substantial exercise and mental stimulation: if you don't have a lot of time and energy to give to your dog, don't get a gundog; it's unfair to the animal.

The terriers are renowned for their energy and spunk. Created originally to "go to ground" against such varmint as badger and fox, terriers are typically feisty small-sized dogs with a lot of heart and absence of fear. Because of their small size, terriers are chosen by many people as apartment and small-home dogs. While these dogs will physically fit well into the smallest home, their temperament and need for exercise demand either frequent romps and outings or a large backyard. A few members of the terrier group are the Fox Terrier, Jack Russell Terrier, Cairn Terrier, as well as the larger Airedale, Soft Coated Wheaten, and Welsh Terriers. Such specifically companion terriers as the Yorkshire, West Highland White, and Toy Fox Terriers are placed in the toy group and make undeniably good small-home and apartment dogs.

The toys are the breeds bred solely as companions—and, of course, as showdogs. The toy dogs are all small, including the smallest, the Chihuahua, and the not too small French Bulldog and Italian Greyhound. Other than the feature of size and their far-reaching appeal as companions, the toy breeds have relatively little in common. The toys pull their members from the other groups already discussed, including the Pomeranian from the nordic breeds, the Papillon from the gundogs, and the Lhasa Apso from the herding group. Many toy dogs have been dubbed "yappy" and "skittish," but these terms are mere prejudices. In truth, the toy group offers

such a wide range of type and personality that no one generalization would suffice to describe this group.

The preceding paragraphs provide but a hint to the world of dogs and the possibilities that await the potential purchaser. Before you buy your dog, the author encourages you to research the group(s) or breed(s) which you find most appealing, most suited to your needs and provisions as an owner. The groupings employed in the preceding paragraphs

A beautiful pair of Golden Retriever puppies. Not infrequently, people will purchase two dogs so that the animals can be companions to each other.

13

important characteristics. By far the definitive source of the dogs of the world, which too employs a categorization similar to this one, is *The Atlas of Dog Breeds of the World*, by Bonnie Wilcox, DVM, and Chris Walkowicz, which is recommended to all dog owners, potential and seasoned veterans alike.

differ from those used by the AKC, KCGB, and other major registering bodies. The reason is that the above-employed groupings are geared towards providing a feasible way of understanding and communicating the breeds of the world based on their

LICENSING AND REGISTRATION

All dogs must be licensed under the specific codes and laws of the respective city in which you live. Additionally, some counties and states may also have codes or laws under which you may fall as a dog owner. All dog owners should contact the governing body of the city or town in which they live for the specifics as they apply to dog owners.

All purebred dogs should be registered with a canine governing body that recognizes the breed of which it is a member. Not every kennel club recognizes every dog breed. For example, the American Kennel Club recognizes just over 100 of the world's 400-plus breeds. Owners of "rare" purebreds and other purebred dogs not recognized by a given kennel club are encouraged to seek out a registry that accepts their breed. The breeder of the dog you purchased should of course

A pair of Siberian Husky puppies. Members of this strikingly handsome breed have a distinguished heritage as rugged, hardworking sled dogs. Owner, Carolyn S. Duryea.

be able to supply you with this information. The reason for registering your dog is that in so doing you are providing important information to associations that work for the betterment, success, and continuation of the breed.

Additionally, becoming active in a breed club or other member organization is recommended to all dog owners. These clubs bring dogs and dog lovers together, and work for the best of the breed, or non-breed as the case may be.

Puppy's Needs

In all cases possible, learn the needs of your puppy prior to purchase. Have handy all necessary provisions, such as crates, beds, feeding dishes and water bowls, before bringing the pup home. In this way, the puppy enters a calm and comfortable new environment: the owner is sure and at ease

A Bichon Frise pup embodying all the charms of puppyhood. The attention and affection that you give to your puppy are the foundation for raising a dog that will be your loyal, trustworthy companion. Owner, Mrs. Judith L. Hilmer.

knowing what to expect from the new puppy and what the new puppy needs.

The requisites of proper puppy upbringing entail the satisfaction of both the basic needs (food, water, shelter, chewing, veterinary care) and the higher needs (socialization, acceptance, and pack assimilation). The psychologist Abraham Maslow takes credit for the formulation of a hierarchy of needs, which uses as its central belief that one cannot advance to a more conscious or intellectual task until the basic needs of the body are satisfied. Of course, Maslow's theory is quite elaborate as applied to human beings, but we can use his main idea to assume that a dog cannot become well socialized if its basic needs are not met, and that an unsociable dog cannot learn or be trained well.

FEEDING THE PUPPY WELL

Properly feeding the pup involves providing essential nutrients to meet the demands of a rapidly growing animal. That you are feeding a sufficient diet is most clearly seen in the pup's general appearance and behavior. A well-fed puppy reveals strength, suppleness of limb, playfulness and abounding energy, good sleeping habits, and— importantly—a good appetite. Remember that every breed is different; some have typically higher metabolisms than others; some are generally more energetic. This fact of difference carries over to the individual members of the breed as well. Therefore, the best founded rule for general prescription feeding is: feed quality dog foods, commercial or a proven recipe, and gauge the amount to feed based upon the physical appearance and behavior of the puppy.

Regarding the specific diet to feed the new pup, it is best (if not imperative) to continue feeding the same (exact) foods that the breeder or pet shop fed, and to continue the same feeding schedule. If you are not provided automatically with the puppy's diet and feeding schedule, ask the seller and he will gladly pass it to you. In a way, having to follow the seller's feeding routine is ideal for the new owner: even if it were not necessary, feeding an already proven diet eliminates the high-risk trial-and-error that would inevitably follow the owner's search for a suitable puppy feed.

The fact that necessitates continuing the seller's feeding routine is that the puppy's digestive system carries a high potential for volatility at this time. Weaned for only a short period, the puppy is not fully acclimated to solid food. Changing diets, especially in a radical manner, can release the puppy's great propensity for diarrhea, constipation, and/or vomiting. Of course, changing the diet is necessary: the soft moist foods of puppyhood will soon be replaced by dry kibbles and canned foods specially designed for adult dogs.

After about five days in the new home, the puppy can be changed gradually to a new diet by adding small quantities of new food to its staple bowl-fillers. For example, if your 10-week puppy is eating six ounces of moistened brand-A three times a day, begin changing his diet (to the preferred food) by reducing the brand-A ration to five ounces and mixing one ounce of the preferred brand for the first day's meals. Feed day one's rations also on the second day. On day three, reduce brand-A ration by an additional ounce, adding another ounce of the preferred brand. Use day three's ration also on day four. Continue the process, observing your dog's bowel movements.

A very hungry group of Beagle youngsters. If you have several puppies, it is fine to let them share their food bowl, provided that each one gets his fair share.

Loose stools and straining during bowel movements can signal too rapid a change in diet or a diet insufficient for the puppy's needs. In these cases, revert to the previous ration in which more of brand-A was included—or adapt the diet to provide for the dog's needs. When stools return to normal, begin again changing the diet—keeping in mind any adaptations that may have been necessary. Should the adverse condition be prolonged, contact the veterinarian.

Consistency in meal time is as important as consistency of meal content in the early days of doghood. Meals should be provided according to a regular (even strict) schedule, again following the one the breeder established and pet shop followed. Along lines similar to changing content, schedule can be altered—perhaps a half-hour a day until the desired time is reached. Though the pup will adjust (usually by going hungry) better gastro-intestinally to change in schedule than to change in content, keeping the schedule change as gradual as possible reduces unnecessary discomfort to the puppy.

Many owners query the quality of commercial puppy and dog foods. The dog food industry has expended and still expends large sums determining the dog's nutritional needs and how to serve them in a palatable form. Commercial dog food companies in general offer quality products worthy of ingestion by show champions and "rug muckers" alike. Which brand? is a question deserving a highly subjective answer. Surely the opinions of your seller and local pet shop proprietor are worthy of consideration, but as long as the nutrients (as listed on the package or supplied by the company) meet the quality standards you and your dog demand, the choice is yours. It must be remembered that such "foods" as biscuits and treats generally have little nutritional value and can spoil your puppy's appetite for the foods it needs. Treats and biscuits should be reserved for puppies who eat their meals well and show signs of nutritional health. The smart owner reserves treats for rewards, using them to shape the dog's behavior to desired ends. Natural bones are best left out of the puppy's diet, as they can cause gastro-intestinal upsets and blockage.

WEEK-BY-WEEK FEEDING

The youngest puppies purchased and brought to new homes are between six and 12 weeks of age. Puppies younger than six weeks have not been weaned from their mother long enough and may not have all their inoculations to protect them in the outside world. Between six and 12 weeks, puppies require four square meals a day, typically created with warm, moistened puppy chow supplemented with milk, yogurt, vitamins, brewers yeast or any other supplement fed and recommended by the breeder or pet shop proprietor. A puppy's food must contain high percentages of protein, vitamins and minerals, and must be easy to digest. Vegetables and other foods rich in complex carbohydrates are not easy for the pup to digest.

When your puppy reaches its 12th week, three sound meals a day should suffice its needs and appetite. This feeding schedule should continue until about five-months age. During this time the bowl should contain

moist or semi-moist puppy food with a few spoons of canned food, or boiled meat if preferred, and vitamin, mineral, and/or any other supplements recommended by the puppy's veterinarian.

By their fifth month, most puppies are ready to try two nutritious meals a day. These meals typically should be larger than the three meals fed earlier and contain a greater percentage of canned or "adult type" foods. Some puppies are a little slower than other to mature. If the pup still requires three meals for a while, it is fine. The most important feeding barometer is your dog's appearance and

A balanced nutritious diet will be reflected in the quality of your puppy's coat.

behavior: a happy, energetic dog— neither too thin nor heavy—is the ideal to see. At this time the young dog is experiencing stunning growth. It is important that the diet contain plenty of calcium, protein, vitamins and other nutrients. A good idea is to schedule another veterinary check-up for this time to have the vet examine the general condition of the pup and to recommend protein, vitamin or other supplements if necessary. Regardless of the countless feeding charts found, there really is no general specific rule regarding the amount of food to feed a dog: if the dog is thin and forever hungry, increase its rations; if heavy and lethargic, the level of exercise should be increased and the rations decreased; if both the rations and exercise levels seem appropriate to the owner and the young dog still experiences a weight problem, contact a veterinarian.

Most breeds attain relative physical maturity sometime around one year. At this time their growth will slow and then cease. However, all dogs, especially the large breeds, will continue to add girth and substance for several more months. High-quality protein is therefore vital at this time.

American Pit Bull Terriers, adult and puppies. It is important that your pet's diet include the correct balance of carbohydrates, proteins, and fats.

Adult dogs, dogs over one year old, must be weaned to adult dog food. Weaning to adult food is very similar to weaning the puppy to a new diet, as already discussed—gradual additions of new food (adult food) to the staple trace the best course. The same digestive reactions must be guarded against. If the dog shows signs such as diarrhea or constipation, revert to the previous ration and continue until the condition cures or veterinary advice is acquired.

Twice-a-day feeding, with one good-sized meal and one smaller meal, is best for most mature dogs. Determining whether the larger meal is given in the morning or evening is left to the owner and the dog. Like some people, some dogs have more zest for a breakfast, while others have more zing for supper. Unless a once-a-day feeding schedule is absolutely necessary, the twice-a-day method is preferred by most canine nutritionists. However, provided your dog receives a complete, well-balanced diet, he should adapt to any normal feeding routine.

As a final note on feeding, no dog requires a diet ranging broadly in palatal stimulation, for the canine sense of taste is much less refined than the human's. This fact can be well substantiated by taking a good look and sniff of the nutritious substance that fills most dog food cans, which by the way tastes just wonderful to dogs. The essential factor is providing good nutrition in a sound, well-balanced diet. Frequent fluctuations and changes in diet lead to fussy eaters and dogs with digestive upsets. The pleasure of eating to the dog comes from the full stomach following consumption, not the tastebud-awakening aroma. Choose the best possible dog food, ideally with assistance from a veterinarian, local breeder, or pet shop proprietor, and feed it consistently.

WATER

Water should be provided to the housebroken dog at all times. For the young puppy, water is best provided at regularly scheduled times—at least six times a day, and certainly after each meal. At each watering time, the pup should be allowed to drink to its full, and then, of course, taken out to relieve itself. Water

"Frequent fluctuations and changes in diet lead to fussy eaters and dogs with digestive upsets."

should never be refused to a thirsty pup, but water constantly provided will inhibit the house-breaking process unless constant supervision is available.

All dogs do not have the same basic water requirements. Large dogs are better able to store water and can therefore go longer periods without a drink, if necessary. Small dogs typically have less ability to store water, requiring that they always have water available. Because most working breeds are larger dogs, forever providing water in the field is not a plaguing concern. However, regular water provision is definitely a concern of small-dog owners who prepare to travel with their dog: an adequate supply of water should be taken for the trip. Puppies cannot store adequate supplies of water for prolonged periods without drink. Elderly dogs very often demand high quantities of water, which aides their aging digestive system and kidneys. Older dogs must have water provided at all times or at least frequently and regularly.

A PLACE TO STAY: CRATES AND BEDS

Every puppy—and indeed every dog—needs a warm, dry place to retire. All canines need a resting place to call their own. If your dog is to be a kennel dog, then his kennel, which should be his own and not shared with another dog, is his private abode. The kennel must be cleaned daily and ideally should provide a place of exercise and leisure. Additionally, all kennel dogs require hours of daily human attention if they are to remain well socialized and disciplined. If your dog is to be an indoor companion, crates and beds need consideration as resting places for the dog.

Ideal for the puppy is the crate or canine carrier. When the pup matures (is housebroken) a dog bed may be more desirable. Dog crates come in many styles, shapes, colors and sizes. The crate also doubles as a carrier for travel.

Indeed, responsible owners will use a crate whenever they bring their dog in the car, on the train, or when travelling by plane—including the first trip home. The crate is recommended for puppies for it greatly assists in the housebreaking process. Besides, if you need a crate for travelling, why not increase its mileage by using it as an early bed for the pup?

The best crate for the puppy is made of sturdy plastic, with an open front grate that latches securely shut. Ventilation is an essential feature, so be sure the crate allows air passage through at least two of its sides. You will probably have to purchase two crates—one for the puppy and one for the adult dog—unless your breed is a particularly small one. Do not buy a crate that is too large, one that "the puppy will grow into." A crate that is too large is one that allows the pup to defecate on one side and stretch out comfortably at the other. This crate will impede the housebreaking process and is not as safe for the puppy when travelling.

Perhaps the worst way to house the puppy is by attaching it to a spike and chain—even if

supplemented with a dog house. Repeated studies by leading authorities on canine behavior state that dogs housed on a chain evidence lesser intelligence, more anti-social temperaments, and behavior problems such as chronic barking to a much higher degree than dogs housed in appropriate kennels and indoors. People interested in this aspect of dog keeping can acquire information in the various canine journals and books about dog behavior and psychology. Ian Dunbar's *Dog Behavior* is an excellent source of such information.

PUPPIES CHEW

Chewing stems from instincts and the inherent need of the pup to chew. Chewing provides comfort during the teething process, helps maintain the puppy teeth, assists in cutting

A trio of Cocker Spaniel puppies. Every dog needs a place that he can call his own, a place in which he can relax and rest.

the primary teeth, strengthens the jaws and facial muscles, relieves doggie tensions, and controls plaque and tartar accumulation. Chewing is a normal, healthy activity, which cannot and should not be thwarted.

Puppies typically go through two teething periods: at 16 weeks, when the permanent teeth begin to emerge, and at eight months, when the molars break through the gums. During these periods the need to chew and gnaw increases, becoming almost constant at times. At all other times the need to chew is still present although less apparent.

Because of puppies' proclivity to chew furniture, shoes—indeed almost anything—the chewing instinct must be directed at an early age to objects that are safe and beneficial to chew. These objects must be readily available to the pup—and mature dog—at all times. Many different types of chew products are available to the owner, but selecting only the safe and effective chew devices is of utmost importance to the well-being of the pup.

Chew toys made of rubber pose the threat of pieces breaking off and being ingested by the pup, causing gastro-intestinal disturbance at best and death by obstruction or asphyxiation at worst. "Squeaky" toys, besides being commonly made of rubber, double the danger by including the squeak device, which dogs almost inevitably remove from the toy base and ingest. Rawhide, though common, is not without definite risks: dogs can tear and swallow pieces too large to be easily digested, causing disturbance and/or obstruction; and some studies indicate the presence of toxic substances in rawhide, with a greater incidence of toxicity in hides originating in third-world countries. Natural bones are often too hard and abrasive for the canine's teeth. Additionally, they commonly cause blockage in the intestines and can splinter, injuring the mouth, esophagus, or the rest of the digestive tract.

To the author's knowledge, the safest and most provenly effective canine chew products are the Nylabone and Gumabone chew devices. These chewing devices are made of annealed nylon and heat-treated polymers respectively and are clinically proven to prevent accumulation of tartar and plaque on the dog's teeth. Considering that plaque is the root cause of periodontitis, the leading cause of gum disease in dogs, the preventive nature of

Nylabone®, the original nylon chew toy, is the perfect puppy pacifier. Proven to outlast other chew toys, Nylabone® helps the pup through the teething period and later becomes the ideal vehicle to vent adult frustrations.

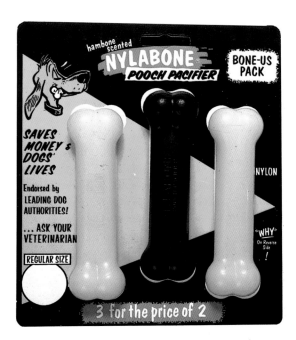

Even if your pup appears to be the picture of perfect canine health, he still needs regular veterinary check-ups. Owner, Dee Schindler.

these products is an undoubtedly important feature. Also, the products come in various sizes for different sized dogs. For puppies, one of the Gumabone products is probably best, due to their softer composition. Puppies never should be given an old shoe, sock, or household object as a chew device: not only can these throwaways be dangerous but they can also confuse the puppy about appropriate objects to chew.

VETERINARY CARE

Every dog needs a veterinarian. The veterinarian, more so than any other person in the dog's world, can properly diagnose and treat problems and conditions of the dog. Veterinarians can even prescribe diets and exercise plans that will help your pup be the best he possibly can be.

Before purchasing the puppy, check its veterinary records; be sure that all its inoculations are up-to-date and that the puppy was generally examined and approved by the inspecting veterinarian. Be sure that there is a clause in your buyer's contract which states that if the pup is not approved by your own chosen veterinarian that the puppy may be returned for full refund until a given time elapses after the initial purchase. Then take the puppy to your chosen vet as soon as possible and have it inspected.

Ask the seller for a copy of the puppy's health record and bring it to the vet on the first visit. Keep a record for yourself and keep it up to date. The puppy's inoculation schedule should read something like this: *canine distemper*, 6–8 weeks, and again at 3 months; *infectious canine hepatitis*, 3 months; *canine parainfluenza*, 3 months; *canine leptospirosis*, 3 months; *rabies*, 6 months, and yearly booster. Additionally, there are numerous other shots and yearly boosters that your veterinarian will explain and recommend, depending on your location and the individual puppy.

In addition to the early visits to the vet, it is best to schedule two regular check-ups annually. At these times the vet will likely ask for a stool sample and possibly a blood test. Stool samples and blood tests are the surest ways to diagnose such hazardous infections and infestations as heartworm, hookworm, infectious canine hepatitis, and numerous other diseases and conditions. At these regular visits the veterinarian will also give your dog a general review and inspect its overall condition. Regular veterinary care is one of the essential basic needs of all puppies and dogs.

THE HIGHER NEEDS

The higher needs of the dog are acceptance, socialization, and pack assimilation. Though each need is unique, they actually intertwine: a dog that feels accepted and welcome most often is well socialized, and a well-socialized dog almost inevitably finds its place in the pack, human and dog.

The canine's need for acceptance begins in early puppyhood, typically around the 13th day of life. At this time the puppy begins its first relationships with its dam and littermates. These relationships build, and from the third through fifth weeks of life

Give the new member of your family time to adjust to his new environment.

social interaction with littermates is vital to the mental soundness of the pup. This early socialization not only serves the pup's early need for acceptance but also commences the need for growing social intercourse. This primary need for acceptance is almost always met by the instinctive canine family. Orphaned pups should not be raised singly but always with their littermates or at least with other puppies.

As the puppy grows, the needs of acceptance and socialization also grow and take new direction. Sometime shortly after the fifth week of life the puppy begins the human socialization period. During this time interaction with humans can shape and mold the future personality of the pup. Acceptance is vital: the pup must feel welcome in the human family and an important part of it. After about 12 weeks of age, the puppy enters a new period, called the juvenile period. It is at this time that one can truly tell how well the puppy's needs for acceptance and socialization were met. The well-provided puppy has little problem fitting into the new home as a new pet. It sees the human family clearly and understands its role as the canine part of it. In other words, it finds its personal niche in the pack, satisfying its ancient pack instinct and satisfying one of dogs' higher needs.

TERRITORY AND DOMINANCE

Canines by nature are territorial and behave largely on the basis of dominance and submission. The territorial aspect extends less to interpack relationships than it does to pack-to-pack and individual-to-foreign-pack relationships. In other words, a dog tends to be less territorial with its immediate family (humans and other house dogs included) than with strangers, strange dogs, and other animals. Of course, territoriality varies from breed to breed and from individual to individual. This book cannot begin to detail the various ways in which territoriality is expressed; however, the new owner should be aware of its presence and supplement his awareness with reading on the temperament of the given breed that he has chosen to own.

Dominance is different than territoriality, as it plays a role not only in pack-to-pack and individual-to-foreign-pack relationships but also has a primary function in interpack interaction. Indeed, the pack itself is founded on a definite hierarchy. The pack leader is inevitably the most dominant member of the group, though not necessarily the largest or strongest member. What makes a pack leader, what makes one dominant, from the canine point of view is often a coupled physical presence and inherent attitude. The dominant one is dominant by nature: dauntless, intelligent, and a born leader. In the pet home, the human should always be the pack leader. Dominance, like territoriality, varies in intensity and direction from breed to breed and individual to individual. It too is expressed in ways too numerous for this book to begin to discuss thoroughly. Again, the owner

Akita pup and his companion. A puppy can be delightfully demonstrative in expressing his affection for his human family.

31

must be aware of its presence, especially if his dog is one among the guardian breeds, and is encouraged to increase his knowledge about this vital canine factor though reading literature about dominance and the basic temperament of his breed.

SUMMING UP THE NEEDS OF THE PUPPY

The needs of all puppies can be divided into two basic, general groups: the basic needs and the higher needs. Each is as equally important as the other to the general well-being of the puppy, and in turn the dog. The basic needs include the needs for food, water, shelter, chewing, and veterinary care, while the higher needs include those of acceptance, socialization, and pack assimilation. These needs are not isolated requisites of proper dog care but are each intertwined, each affecting the other: a poorly fed dog inevitably chews more, requires more veterinary care and is difficult to train, making it poorly socialized and in turn an alien in the pack. Dogs want nothing more than to please man, their masters. Eliciting this primary, inherent desire is not difficult: meet the needs of the dog, and the dog will meet your every need for and expectation of a canine.

You should be fully aware of all the responsibilities that go along with dog ownership before you purchase that very special puppy.

GROOMING AND GENERAL HYGIENE

Grooming should not be seen as an arduous task, for it can be a most rewarding, enjoyable experience for both you and your dog. If performed regularly, following a prescribed method, grooming becomes a simple procedure that allows excellent human-to-canine interaction and provides results that are immediately pleasing. No dog looks and feels its best unless properly groomed, and no owner takes more pride than in seeing his canine friend look and feel downright awesome.

The owner must be aware that each breed has special grooming needs: some require extensive clipping, others no clipping at all; some stripping, others a simple once-over with a hound glove and turkish towel. Essentially, all dogs require a daily brushing. Long-coated dogs typically fare best under the strokes of either a natural bristle, pin, or wire brush (depending on the breed),

Bichon Frise pup. Owner, Mrs. Judith L. Hilmer.

while the short-coated breeds often prefer a hound glove or curry brush and metal comb (again depending on the breed). Truly to achieve the most outstanding dog possible, the dog owner should acquire a breed-specific grooming handbook and follow its prescribed procedure. Of course, professional groomers are more than happy to provide their services to all dog owners. If grooming is not a practice for you, have your dog visit a professional groomer regularly.

As was said, grooming affords great opportunity for interaction with your dog. If begun at an early age, which all grooming procedures should, grooming is more than accepted by the dog. Your dog will come to enjoy the time spent with you and the skin-tingling stimulation of brushes and combs. When the day's grooming is over, your dog will feel refreshed and will perceive your effort as performed for its own sake, not your own. In return, your dog will likely reward you with renewed affection and admiration. Yet, this great interaction is but a beneficial byproduct to a most necessary process. Regular grooming keeps the skin and coat clean and healthy, removing debris and dead skin cells, distributing natural oils, and guarding against parasites and skin infections.

Tools needed by the groomer vary depending on the breed and the degree to which it is to be groomed. A specialized text on your breed that includes a prescribed grooming method will inform you on which tools you need. In general, pet shops carry all the grooming tools you will need, so there is no worry or hassle over finding and ordering odds and ends with which to groom your dog.

Bathing

Bathing is an essential part of good grooming habits. Unlike brushing, bathing is never a daily ritual. Most dog require full-scale baths only three to four times a year. Many dogs, such as most indoor dogs, require bathing only once or twice a year. As a general rule, bathing is best performed as *infrequently* as necessary. The dog's skin and coat simply cannot withstand the oil depletion that results from frequent bathing, as dogs' oil glands are much fewer in number than humans'. Additionally, a puppy younger than six months of age should never be bathed; its delicate, sensitive skin and coat stand poorly under the lather of a *dog*

If you are uncertain about how to properly use a given grooming tool, check with a professional groomer. You certainly wouldn't want to make a "mistake" that will mar your pet's coat.

standard shampoos while others are designed to fight fleas and ticks, dry skin and coat, or to deodorize the dog. Use the product that best fits your dog's needs. Do not use a medicated shampoo if your dog has no medicinal needs, for a standard shampoo and conditioner will likely result in better coat condition. Besides shampoos and conditioners, there are other canine-coat products available, including tangle-free rinses and separate skin and coat conditioners. These products, like the specialized shampoos, can be of great assistance to keeping your dog properly groomed and should be used as necessary.

There is no one single all-encompassing way to bathe all dogs. As with clipping and brushing, the way to bathe a given dog depends largely on its breed and temperament. Surely bathing a nine-pound Cocker Spaniel requires a different procedure than bathing a 90-pound corded-coat Komondor, and the owner is encouraged to acquire a breed-specific grooming guide for their dog. There are, however, a few basics that apply to nearly every bathing procedure, and they are

shampoo. If the puppy becomes exceedingly soiled, a sponge bath, using only warm water and no soap, can be given. In extreme cases, contact a professional groomer or veterinarian for a bathing procedure specially prescribed for your puppy's condition.

Because the dog's skin and coat is much different than our own, it only makes sense to bathe the dog with products specially designed for canines, not humans. There is an abundance of such type products available at local pet shops and veterinary offices. These products are both affordable and specially suited to fulfill the canine's bathing needs.

Dog shampoos come in many different kinds: some are simply

provided here for the reader.

First. Begin bathing the puppy at about one year of age to accustom it to the bathing process. Waiting until the dog is two or three years of age could result in a fierce, frightful struggle in the tub. Younger dogs are typically more open to new experiences than are older dogs.

Second. Always brush the coat well before bathing. Brushing helps to loosen dirt, debris, and dead hairs, which may otherwise be left behind after the bath. Also, if the dog has any mats, they should be broken up before the bath. Bathing will certainly only make the matted condition of the dog worse.

Third. Be sure that the dog is secured in the tub. A nylon leash secured firmly to a post is recommended. Allowing the dog to jump out of the tub—which it most unhesitatingly will do if given the opportunity—is both dangerous and messy.

Fourth. When bathing large dogs, and all dogs having their first bath, have someone on hand to assist you should the need arise. You may be overwhelmed to find your placid Yorkshire turned gremlin from hell upon being placed in the tub.

Fifth. Be sure that your bathing accommodations are sufficient. Make certain that the tub is large enough and is provided with a non-slip bottom. The water should be warm, not hot or cold, and the product you use should be made specially for dogs.

Lastly. Always start the lather at the head and work towards the tail. After a good lather is worked over the entire dog, be absolutely sure to rinse the lather thoroughly, as left over lather can cause irritation and dandruff. After the thorough rinsing, towel-dry the dog and keep him away from drafts. On warm sunny days he

Shorthaired breeds such as the Beagle do not require elaborate grooming procedures.

37

can be let out to dry, but most freshly bathed dogs have the tendency to role in the first dirt patch they see. Otherwise, the dog should be allowed to dry in the house or be dried with a blow drier, set on low heat to avoid damaging the coat and skin.

CARE OF SPECIAL PARTS

The eyes, ears, nose, and claws are all anatomical parts deserving of special attention by the owner. These parts ideally should be checked every day as part of the daily grooming procedure. The eyes, ears, and nose typically require little more than checking, while the claws will need regular clipping to prevent splayed feet and other foot problems.

Check the eyes for signs of irritation. Common signs include excessive discharge, redness, and cloudiness. The eyes are one of the first indicators of disease and other undesirable conditions; if any of these signs are persistently present, a veterinarian should be consulted. Some breeds are more prone to eye infections and other conditions than other breeds. The responsible owner should read up on eye conditions that commonly affect his breed. Foreign objects can also lodge in or scratch the eyes. Foreign objects must be removed by a veterinarian.

The ears should be checked for irritation, redness, swelling, and excessive wax accumulation. Ear mites are a common parasite of the ear, with most dogs experiencing a mite infestation at least once in their lifetime. The presence of ear mites can usually be determined by a bad-smelling brownish wax build-up in the ear. Upon carefully removing a bit of the wax and smearing it on black paper, the owner can detect tiny reddish, orange, or yellowish mites—often helpful is the assistance of a magnifying glass. Regular accumulations of wax are to be expected and can be removed by wiping the ear with a soft cotton towel moistened with a canine ear-cleaning solution, exercising caution not to probe into the ear canal. Irritation and redness, especially accompanied by soreness, can be a sign of an ear infection. Ear infections are very serious, for if untreated they can quickly spread to the middle and inner ear, possibly resulting in nerve damage and even death. Swelling of the ear leather is usually the sign of a hematoma. Hematomas are often not serious, but, as with all swelling, deserve veterinary care.

The nose should be checked for excessive discharge, dryness, and sunburn. Excessive discharge can signal an upper-respiratory infection or the presence of nasal mites. Chronic dryness too can

When clipping your puppy's claws, avoid clipping the quick, the vein that runs through each claw. Your veterinarian can show you how to correctly perform this procedure.

indicate infection or disease. Chronic sunburn can lead to a condition called Collie nose, which in acute cases can lead to cancer in later age. Dogs that spend a lot of time outdoors should be provided with some form of sun protection.

The dog's claws will grow too long, curling under and splaying the feet, if not properly attended. Unless the dog is provided with ample exercise on hard surfaces, including asphalt, cement, and gravel, the claws will require regular clipping. Clipping the claws is a relatively simple procedure provided that the dog does not object too much. Most important is not cutting off too much of the nail, thus severing the quick. The quick is the area of live veins and blood vessels that run into each claw, feeding the live matter of the claw. Clipping into the quick results in bleeding. This bleeding can be stopped with the application of a styptic powder and pressure. It is best that the new owner ask the veterinarian to perform the first nail-clipping procedure, while the owner watches carefully. The rate at which nails grow varies from breed to breed and individual to individual. In general, weekly checks and a monthly trimming suffice for nail service.

EARLY TRAINING

Early training involves teaching the pup the four basic commands come, sit, lie, and down, as well as conditioning the pup to basic lead training. Learning the basic commands and adjusting to the laws of the lead are as important to the pup as learning his name, which by the way is the completing piece to early training.

The puppy's early training begins his first day in the new home, the first time you call his name. Starting the very first time you address your dog—and continuing every time thereafter—use only the dog's given name, the name you chose for the dog. Addressing the dog in a variety of names or a myriad of ever-slightly-changing nicknames will eventually confuse the animal and possibly lead to training problems, especially in the advanced stages of training.

COME
The come and the sit commands are possibly the

easiest of all to teach and are often the first commands the puppy learns. The owner should begin conditioning the puppy to the come command the first day home: each time you are setting the pup's food dish on the floor for the pup, state in an authoritative tone "Come." Do this also whenever you have a toy or treat to give the dog, or later when the lead is taken out of the closet to take the dog for a walk. State the come command every time you have something pleasing to give to the pup and he is not immediately nearby—telling a dog that is by your feet to come will not teach the dog anything and will likely confuse it. By hearing the come command often and associating it with pleasing rewards, the puppy will be well conditioned to master the come command. The polishing stages involve providing the dog distractions, such as other people, dogs, or play things, and commanding the dog to come to you. When he does, warm, lavish praise, and possibly a treat (especially helpful in the early stages) should be given as reward: the dog must be let to know that it did good by coming to you. If

distractions are too much for the dog to overcome, the dog is not yet conditioned enough to the command. Continue, perhaps with more frequency, the primary conditioning phases (feeding dish, favorite toy, etc.). Many puppies learn the come command even before they begin the housebreaking process (three to four months).

SIT

The sit command is similarly easy to teach, and it too can begin the first day you bring the pup home. What makes teaching this command easy is a basic understanding of the dog's physiology. Because of the construction of the neck and spine, it is not easy for a dog to look upward. The observant owner will notice that a dog will sit to look a standing person in the eye and will sit to see an object placed on a table or stand. To condition the dog to the sit command, begin by holding objects that are appealing to the dog in a raised hand. When the standing dog dog catches view of the object, give the sit command in an authoritative tone as the dog sits to attain a better, easier view. As soon as the dog sits, give the object and praise. Because sitting is so natural a habit for the dog, it may take longer for the dog to associate the command with the action. However, consistency will pay off soon, and the dog will inevitably associate the command with the action, and in turn the action with the pleasing reward.

After the dog learns the come command, the come and sit commands can be coupled: the dog can be called at meal time and, before the meal is placed down, made to sit by holding the food dish in the hand and commanding "Sit." Thus the meal can serve as dual reward for both the come and sit compliance. Of course, come and sit can be coupled with any reward, including a toy, treat, or simple praise. Praise, warm and lavish, is one of dog's favorite rewards.

LIE

The lie command is similar to the sit command, except that the puppy does not lie to see things better but rather to relax and retire. Teaching the lie command involves good observation. As is the case with sitting, lying is a natural action,

and it may take the dog a few weeks of consistently hearing the command in conjunction with his action to begin to understand the command. Whenever the pup begins to lie down, state "Lie" in a firm voice. As soon as the dog lies, give him warm praise. It is best to say simply "Lie" and not "Lie down," for when the down command is taught some confusion may result. Once you think the puppy understands the command, you can test his learning by giving the command when the pup shows no signs of

You can begin your puppy's training program the first day he arrives at your home. If you are patient and consistent, the positive results of your efforts should be readily apparent by the time your pet reaches adulthood.

lying down. At first it is best not to have distractions present, but as the command becomes more firmly implanted distractions can be presented to increase the training. As with all training procedures, successful compliance by the dog deserves immediate reward.

DOWN

The down command is certainly more difficult to teach the puppy than the first three, more basic commands. Nonetheless, the down command is an essential one for the puppy to learn. A puppy that jumps on people and furniture is often a nuisance, and this behavior can negatively affect the person-to-pet relationship. Unlike the previous three commands, where the owner is using the natural behavior of the puppy to teach training, the down command involves breaking the puppy of an almost instinctive habit.

Several different methods are proposed by various authorities on canine training. Some involve more force and punishment, while others rely on quick reflexes and praise. Because the author believes that observation and praise can train any dog, the latter type training is presented. Teaching the down command can be very easy if the puppy is never rewarded for jumping up. It may sound too primitively obvious, but in too many cases owners condone

undesirable behavior of a dog because it seems cute of a puppy. Granted, a six-pound puppy jumping on one's shin may not trouble anyone, but as the puppy grows and as the behavior becomes more persistent, jumping becomes annoying. Stopping a dog from jumping who was allowed to jump as a puppy is incredibly more difficult than teaching a puppy not to jump from the time it enters the new home.

The key to teaching the down command then is not allowing

The command to have your pet offer his paw may be a bit more difficult for him to master, compared to some of the other commands.

Most puppies are eager to please. Make the most of this canine quality by offering lavish praise to your pet when he correctly responds to a given command.

the puppy up. When the puppy comes to greet you or to play, watch closely that it stops in front of you and makes no motion to jump on you. If the pup makes motion to jump, time its jump with a quick step backwards. The pup will have nothing to plant on and will return to the standing position. Give the down command quickly and sharply as the pup "falls" back to the standing position. As soon as the puppy is in the position, give warm praise. All members of the household, as well as frequent guests, should be informed of this procedure and follow it. If just one person allows the pup to jump, then the training process can be made considerably more difficult.

Jumping on furniture requires a little more "hands-on" training. Watch the puppy. As soon as it jumps on the furniture, take its forepaws—or the entire puppy if it is completely atop the furniture—and return them (or it) swiftly to the ground while commanding "Down" in a clear, sharp voice. As soon as the puppy is returned to the floor, give lavish praise. Again, all members of the household should be informed of this practice. Whenever observation is not possible, the puppy should be kept in its chosen play area or crate, where there is not furniture on which to jump.

LEAD TRAINING

All puppies should become accustomed to the collar and lead at an early age, eight to ten weeks. The collar comes first and should be put on the puppy as soon as possible, thus allowing the attachment of a name tag, vaccination tag, and license. The best collar for a puppy is made of either soft leather or nylon. It should fit comfortably around the neck, not too loose to be pulled over the head or too tight that it will pinch the skin. The puppy may struggle and strain a bit, maybe even whimper, when the collar is first put on. Soon, however, he will adjust fine. In a day or two, the puppy will not even realize it has a collar on.

After the pup is well acclimated to the feel of the

collar, try attaching a lead to it. Allow the pup to run around freely with the collar dragging behind. Let the pup sniff, bite and paw at the lead, thus coming to know that it is a harmless object. These lead acclimating periods should be done a few times a day for two to three days before actual lead training begins.

Lead training commences with the puppy's first walk on the lead. Some experts believe that the first walks should actually be taken in the home, the area with which the pup is most familiar. The author sees merit in the idea but believes that such is not necessary. During the first few walks, allow the pup to lead you.

Stamina and endurance can vary greatly from breed to breed. Keep this in mind when planning your pet's training program.

Apply gentle but firm restraint and never pull or jerk the puppy. After a few walks, the puppy will learn and appreciate the restrictions of the lead.

The first lead training lesson involves teaching the puppy to heel. Before beginning this and other lead training lessons, it is usually best that the pup has mastered the aforementioned basic commands, such as come, sit, and stay. Lead training is not only more difficult for the pup but often uses these basic commands during the lessons.

Begin the heel lesson with the pup sitting on your left side, collar and lead attached. Hold the end of the lead in your right hand and the middle of the lead in your left hand, forming a visual J-loop. Place your left hand, palm facing the puppy, in front of the puppy's nose. When ready, raise your left hand and firmly give the command "Heel" while beginning the walk with your left foot first. For the first few (even many) lead training lessons the pup will inevitably attempt to prance in front of you. However, the object of training to heel is to

Five-month-old Great Dane. Even the most well-trained dog may wander off if something captures his attention. Always supervise your pet when he is outdoors.

keep the dog walking even with your left side. Therefore, when the pup lunges forward, give a quick, sharp tug at the lead while commanding "Heel." The tug is not to lift the pup into the air or cause pain but simply to bring the pup to associate discomfort with lunging in front during a walk. As soon as the pup is brought back to the side of the walker, praise and reward (verbal and/or other) should be given. The key to teaching the heel lesson is persistence, consistency and praise. Do not get disheartened after six or even 12 unsuccessful lessons. Keep the lessons short, about 15 minutes at most, and perform them several times a day, three to four being ideal. Many pups take several weeks of such training, but the end result is well worth the effort: the heel command is the most basic

lead-training command and the command upon which all future lead training is built.

SUMMING UP EARLY TRAINING

The lessons and commands just covered in this chapter are the basic training which every puppy should have. A puppy untrained in these basics can become both a nuisance and a hazard as a dog. Additionally, the author encourages all dog owners to seek additional obedience training after their dog reaches six or so months of age. Obedience classes are best attended by both owner and dog and assist greatly in solidifying

A pair of Poodle puppies. Pups of the same litter can be quite different in personality.

the human-to-pet bond. Additionally, it should be mentioned that the above-described training methods reflect but one of many different styles of puppy training. While the author believes that these reflect the best school of thought regarding puppy training, all owners who find difficulty training their dog this way are encouraged to seek other training methods.

HOUSEBREAKING

Housebreaking is the delicate process by which the puppy learns where to relieve itself. It is a delicate process because the ramifications of the process can be many and distressing. Essentially, dogs are clean animals, and this cleanliness begins in early puppyhood. No dog, if properly reared, likes a soiled environment: dogs in the wild rarely defecate in or around their den. The same is true for the domestic puppy. If given the choice between soiling its crate and relieving itself elsewhere, the puppy inevitably opts for elsewhere. It is up to the owner, therefore, to direct this inherent desire for cleanliness in the appropriate direction: outdoors or in the litter box.

No puppy can be housebroken before it reaches three to four months of age. Before this time the puppy simply does not have the muscle control necessary to comply with the laws of housebreaking. Attempting to housebreak a pup younger than three months will only lead to frustration for both the owner and animal, and will likely complicate the housebreaking

Successfully housebreaking your puppy requires time, patience, and consistency on your part.

procedure later. The only thing the owner can do with a young pup is watch it carefully, moving it to paper if he sees him ready to execute a no-no and keep the pup in its crate or confined area when observation is impossible. Clean-up must occur as immediately as possible: no puppy or dog should be allowed to inhabit a soiled environment for any time longer than necessary, for doing so greatly hinders the housebreaking process.

CRATE TRAINING

Most specialists assert that crate training is the best method of housebreaking a dog. Crate training demands a little more time and commitment from the owner, but it establishes a more quickly and thoroughly housebroken animal than the long-established method of paper training. Crate training also involves a small financial expenditure, for the owner must invest in a dog crate, or portable kennel, which will serve as the puppy's home through the housebreaking process. As was mentioned in the discussion of the puppy's needs, crates serve many functions, and many modes of travel are prohibited unless the dog is transported in a crate. Therefore, the crate is actually less of a housebreaking expense than a canine necessity.

When you first bring the puppy home, introduce the crate as the puppy's own. Let the pup sniff and explore. Many owners are surprised when the pup wanders right into the crate and retires for a nap. Of course, if the pup was transported home in its crate, this informal introduction is not necessary.

The contents of the crate should include a blanket, towel or other suitable bedding, a safe chew toy, and a few objects which you feel will make the pup feel more pleased with his new home. It is best that you do not clutter the crate but rather let the pup perceive plenty of space in which to stretch out and nap—one of puppy's favorite past-times. The size of the crate is very important: the crate should be large enough for the pup to stand up and move around comfortably without being large enough for the pup to sleep in one section and relieve itself in another, as this too can hinder the housebreaking process.

To crate train the dog the key is routine: the puppy must be allowed out of the crate frequently enough to relieve itself regularly. The basis of crate training relies on the fact that puppies are less likely to soil their immediate environment, an instinct that grows stronger with age. When supervision is present, the door of the crate should be left open and the puppy should be free to enter and exit the crate. The crate should be permanently located in a restricted area, thus preventing the pup from going to a far corner of the house to relieve itself. During supervision the owner must watch carefully for signs that the pup is going to urinate or defecate. At the first sign, the puppy should be quickly, gently picked-up and taken to the chosen place of evacuation. The owner should stay with his dog until it does its business. Immediately following, even during, the pup's business, warm, lavish praise must be given. The puppy must come to know that it is doing good by going at the spot to which the owner brought it. After praise, the puppy can then be returned to its restricted area and allowed to play.

At all times when strict supervision is not possible, the puppy should be locked in the crate. However, the pup must be taken to the chosen area of evacuation regularly, as soon as the owner returns or morning arises. If the pup is left too long in the crate, it will not be able to hold in its excrement and will necessarily soil its crate. In this

Some dog owners prefer to use housebreaking pads, instead of newspaper, to cover their pet's designated bathroom area. These pads provide more absorbency than newspaper.

case a scolding should *not* be given. It is not the pup's fault, and besides the pup does not associate punishment with an action that occurred in the past.

The necessary regimen for successful crate training involves taking the puppy to the chosen spot of evacuation immediately following each feeding, whenever it shows signs of readiness to evacuate, and at regular intervals throughout the day. After a feeding and whenever signs are present, the pup must be kept in the spot until it does its business. Every time the pup goes in the appropriate spot, warm and lavish praise must be given. If the pup goes other than in the desired location it is not its fault but the owner's: young puppies have very limited capacity for holding their excrement, and the owner

simply did not provide adequate opportunity for relief. Through praise for deeds well done and the provision of a clean home quarters, puppies quickly learn the desired location for evacuation. In this way, housebreaking is quickly and thoroughly accomplished.

PAPER TRAINING

Paper training is one of the oldest and most widely used methods of housebreaking. Paper training is simple and proven. However, it does have a few disadvantages: paper training is typically a longer process than crate training and has a higher potential not to fully housebreak a dog. These set-backs are attributed to the fact that paper training primarily takes place within the home, and thus becomes a two-stage process: one, to get the pup to go only on paper, and then two, to get the pup to go only outdoors. The risk of achieving a partially housebroken dog is due to the dog's having learned at first that it is O.K. to go indoors so long as it is on newspaper (or WeeWee pads). Not to mislead the reader, paper training is a relatively good way to housebreak a dog. The owner who opts for this method, however, must be aware of its potential shortcomings. Paper training is best for those owners who do not have the extra time for crate training, which requires consistent outings to a selected spot. Paper training is also ideal for owners of small, solely indoor dogs that will not be let out to relieve themselves. As with crate training, paper training cannot be successful prior to the puppy's third or fourth month of life, as the pup simply does not have the bodily control necessary.

Paper training begins with the selection of a confined area in which the pup will spend most of its time. This area is then lined completely, covering the entire surface, with paper or another chosen medium. Newspaper is most common only because it is inexpensive. Regular observation is important: every time the young pup is seen going on the papers, it should be warmly praised. Additionally, paper training is not a substitute for outdoor training for any but solely indoor dogs. The puppy must still be taken out immediately following meals, whenever it shows signs of preparing to relieve itself, and at regular intervals. If the puppy is not taken out at these times, the housebreaking process is critically slowed.

After the first few days, when the pup realizes that going on the paper and going outdoors is good, the papered area should be diminished gradually, always in the direction of the pup's chosen spot if one is evident. Most pups will have such a spot on the papered area where they prefer to go, but if not the owner can exercise his judgment when determining in which direction the papered area will recede.

Encourage the pup to go only on the papered area with the same type of warm praise used earlier. Additionally, if the pup goes other than on the papered area and is caught in the act, then a brief verbal reprimand may be given. However, if the owner did not actually witness the action and follow it immediately with reprimand then punishment is senseless, futile, and only serves to dishearten the pup. *No* dog should ever have its nose rubbed in the excreta. This is a barbaric practice which serves

"As with crate training, paper training cannot be successful prior to the puppy's third or fourth month of life, as the pup simply does not have the bodily control necessary."

55

no purpose other than to denigrate both the owner and his dog. Praise for correct behavior is always the best way to train a dog at any task. As the papered area continually decreases, it should be moved progressively closer to and finally out the door, at which time the pup should be completely housebroken.

MISHAPS

Mishaps and mistakes seem inevitably to happen. If a mishap occurs, chances are that the dog was not given adequate times to relieve itself and was not allowed to follow the routine as originally established by the owner. If the puppy which *thought* was housebroken soils in the house, it is best to revert back to the housebreaking routine for a week or so. In this case it is likely that the dog was not completely housebroken to begin with. Puppies which "refuse" or cannot be housebroken typically have either a disease or adverse condition, including improper socialization or congenital kidney or bladder disorder. In these cases, veterinary diagnosis is imperative to the well-being of your dog. Of course, a puppy which takes longer than expected to become fully housebroken is not necessarily an impossible dog to housebreak: dogs, like humans, are each individuals, learning and conforming at their own pace.

If the owner has chronic difficulty housebreaking his dog, professional trainers can likely come to assistance.

Sick dogs typically should not become *un*housebroken. Sick dogs do, however, require more time from their owner. A sick dog will require more frequent trips outside, if a specific indoor area is not provided for the duration of the illness, depending, of course, upon the specific disease or condition and its degree of severity. When a sick dog has an accident, the dog typically should not be punished, as it is most often the owner who is not meeting his responsibilities as a dog owner: providing the sick dog with the additional outings that its system needs. A dog suffering with diarrhea will need an ever-present location in which to relieve itself, for bodily control simply is not there.

THE PUPPY

The puppy grows and matures in its first year of life at roughly the equivalent rate to seven years of human development. For the puppy and the owner, this is a time of

discuss better the transformation. The neonatal (birth to 12 days) and transition periods (13 to 20 days) comprise the first three weeks of puppy development.

During its first twelve days the pup is totally dependent on the dam. Puppies are blind, deaf, without teeth, too weak to walk; have poorly developed sense of smell; and lack stored energy to provide their own warmth; at this stage puppies even rely on the dam to stimulate their defecation. During this critical time, pups are subject to disease, poisoning, and other lethal agents; physical defects often take their toll during the first two weeks of life. Until the pup's brain and motor coordination are more developed, the pup's response to stimuli will be slow and ineffective; and until its metabolism stabilizes, feedings must occur with utmost regularity. Typically the dam provides all the puppy's needs at this time, while the breeder assures a warm, dry, clean and safe environment. However, it is the breeder's responsibility to ensure the puppies' safety: keeping them warm and/or

great, rapid change. Basic human understanding of the puppy's first year can greatly smooth any potential rough edges of the person-to-pet relationship.

From birth to 20 days the pup experiences broad awakenings in its sense of self and surroundings. Physical and psychological development are so great that researchers have divided this short period into two parts to understand and bottle feeding if necessary, and protecting against too many visitors and disturbances.

The transition period is a time when the once totally dependent pup starts to experience control over its developing body and begins to recognize its surrounding environment. The transition period is marked by the opening of the pup's eyes and ends with the coming of the startle response, which demonstrates strong development of the brain and motor coordination. The puppy also begins to demonstrate emotional response and can suffer psychologically if the breeder does not adapt his interaction to the once-helpless animal that is now showing hints of maturity. Additionally, the interaction of the pup and the dam and littermates takes new form, becoming recognizable as clear (though primary) socialization. Despite the great strides, however, the puppy is still dependent on the dam for food, warmth, and stimulation; and its sensory perception is yet to be fully developed.

The end of the transition period marks the beginning of the litter socialization period (21 to 35 days). The pup's true awareness of others besides its self and its mother begins, and motifs of its future personality emerge and subside through the day's activities. The pup's nervous and motor development reach further maturity, and voluntary actions take place. Puppies at this stage respond to stimuli and can see and hear. At about four weeks the dam will begin to vomit her food to introduce the pups to semi-

Which one would you choose? With puppies as cute as these, the choice would be difficult.

are very important at this time. A pup that lives in a dirty environment will likely be hard to housebreak and possibly hard to train.

Through interaction with siblings and humans, a social hierarchy is created: inherent dominance will emerge and pups will jockey for the position of pack leader. Through this hierarchical interaction, each pup will learn its contribution to the group, and all puppies will become social beings. What exactly makes a pack leader is not fully understood by canine behaviorists; believably it can be size, strength, stamina, and/or vocal ability, depending, of course, on the breed, the litter size, and the individual litter and dog. The pup's environment at this time should remain relatively unchanged, and direct contact and interaction should be limited to the few people who actually attend to the litter. Time away from the nest should be kept to short intervals. The litter socialization period is a time of great learning potential. Training is futile, however, and must not be attempted.

Weeks five through 12 are called the "human socialization

liquid food, which behavior is critical to development. The pup now becomes a conscious being. Reacting to its environment, the pup startles, whimpers, and sleeps contentedly. The puppy now uses its vocal cords to bark, an important mode of canine communication. Because the pup is aware of its environment, cleanliness as well as acclimatization to noise and other environmental conditions period." Interaction with humans at this time can largely determine the puppy's future within the human pack, and all encounters with humans help shape the puppy's personality. Persons must be gentle, kind, and firm in their communications with pups of this stage, for puppies must grow to love people yet accept and respect human dominance. However, it still is primarily the dam's role to be pack leader and teacher. By eight weeks, the pup's memory is fully developed and most of what it learns at this time will affect all of its future interactions with humans and other animals. Children should be supervised, for a careless, hurtful child can instill a lifelong aloofness or fear of children. Correction should be kept to a minimum: although the pup can learn simple tasks, it has not mastered its muscles and curiosity. The pup will actively explore and learn about its environment. Brain and sensory perception become more acute and emotional reactions are easily observed. The pup should

be free to learn and explore.

During the first half of the human socialization period, the puppy enters its first "fear period," during which strangers, strange sounds, and changes in the environment startle and frighten. The fear period passes quickly, leaving the pup a more secure and self-reliant animal. Another fear period is encountered around eight weeks, and a final one during

Undeniably, bringing up a puppy involves some hard work, but the thrills of enjoying your dog's puppyhood will be worth the effort.

Whippet puppy. A sound diet, regular veterinary check-ups, and your tender loving care will help ensure that your puppy grows up to be a healthy, happy adult dog.

talk gently and soothingly to the animal.

Occurring within the human socialization period is the second transition stage (seven through 12 weeks). Sometime during this period most puppies leave their dam and littermates to make for a new home. Proper rearing can be clearly evident to the new owner: the puppy should demonstrate good muscle and mental ability and a fair degree of self control; the puppy should not fear humans and should be a relatively secure individual. About one week into this second transition stage puppies experience another fear period, at which time it is important to limit changes in the puppy's environment. If weaning was already over by the eighth week, this fear period may have already passed, for it usually corresponds with weaning, in which the dam begins to threaten the pups while they nurse, which in turn carries over to the pup's play and group behavior. During this fear period, puppies learn the rules of dominance and submission and the use of fear and threat display in life.

It is important for the new

the next (juvenile) period. The need and desire to investigate grows stronger every day, with the pup's finding a strange but irresistibly interesting world outside its box. The pup will show interest yet hesitation with people. Between six and seven weeks, most pups receive their first shots, and their experience at the vet is crucial—meeting a strange man in a strange environment, sticking a strange object painfully into the flank can surely leave an inextricable bad impression. Stay with the puppy while at the vet's and owner and breeder to work closely and openly on these matters: while you may strongly desire an eight-week-old pup, it is best to wait until the puppy has passed its fear period. In other words, while seven to 12 weeks is an ideal age at which to purchase a puppy, during the six to 12 days of the fear period is a very bad time to bring the new pup home.

The juvenile period (12 weeks to six months) is a time when all senses develop to their maturity. Emotional maturity usually occurs sometime between the 13th and 16th week, and sexual maturity begins sometime around the 16th week, continuing into adulthood. Male dogs typically begin to mark their territory with urine by their eight month. By the 16th week, the teething process is usually completed, with the permanent teeth (except the molars) peeking well through the gums. The juvenile period is the ideal time for the owner and dog to come to full understandings of each other. The puppy's intelligence, absorption, and activity level are impressive at this time. Basic training and housebreaking should begin in earnest.

Two-month-old Staffordshire Bull Terriers. Owner, Cock 'N' Bull Kennels.

Index